What is Worth While?

What is Worth While?

Anna Robertson Brown Lindsay

Waymark Books

Copyright © 2023 by Cedar Lake Classics

This is a proofread and newly designed edition of a public domain work.

CONTENTS

DEDICATION vi

1 | What is Worth While? 1

SHORT ESSAYS THAT CHANGED THE WORLD 19

"Let but eternity look, more or less visibly, through the Time-Figure."
THOMAS CARLYLE.

1

What is Worth While?

Only one life to live! We all want to do our best with it. We all want to make the most of it. How can we best get hold of it? How can we accomplish the most with the energies and powers at our command? What is worthwhile? We all ask ourselves this question when we leave our college halls. But the first years out of college are apt to be anxious, unsatisfactory, disappointing. Time slips away in further preparation, in experiment, in useless or misdirected efforts. The world does not prove to be the same that it seemed to be in the quiet college surroundings. Duty is not so clear as then, nor work so well-defined. Life is harder to handle than we thought. One finds that theories fail, and yet one has not had positive experience enough to know just where the difficulty lies. It is of a few simple things that "my own life has proved true" that I shall speak to-day.

Life is large. We cannot possibly grasp the whole of it in the few years that we have to live. What is vital? What is essential? What may we profitably let go? Let us ask ourselves these questions to-day.

To begin with, what may we let go? Who shall say? By what standard shall we measure? By what authority decide? Each of us must answer that question for herself. In looking about for an answer, I find only one that satisfies me. It is this: *We may let go all things which we cannot carry into the eternal life.* To me this is a deep truth, and a positive one. Surely it is not worthwhile for us to cumber our lives with the things which we can grasp at best for but a little time, when we may lay hold of things that shall be ours for ten thousand times ten thousand years.

We may drop pretence. Eternity is not good for shams. In its clear light the false selves that we have wrought about us like a garment will shrivel and fall away. Whatever we really are, that let us be, in all fearlessness. Whatever we are not, that let us cease striving to seem to be. If we can rid ourselves of all untruth of word, manner, mode of life and thinking, we shall rid our lives of much rubbish, restlessness, and fear. Let us hide nothing, and we shall not be afraid of being found out. Let us put on nothing, and we shall never cringe. Let us assume nothing, and we shall not be mortified. Let us do and say nothing untrue, and we shall not fear to have the deepest springs of our lives sought out, nor our most secret motive analyzed. Nothing gives such upright dignity of mien as the consciousness, "I am what I pretend to be. About me there is no make-believe."

We may drop worry. The eternal life is serene. It is not careworn, nor knows it any foreboding of future ill. Can we not take to ourselves its large spirit of serenity and cheer? For only the serene soul is strong. Every moment of worry weakens the soul for its daily combat. Worry is an infirmity; there is no virtue in it. Worry is spiritual near-sightedness; a fumbling way of looking at little things, and of magnifying their value. True spiritual vision sweeps the universe and sees things in their right proportion. The finest landscape of Corot viewed asquint, or out of focus, would appear distorted and untrue. Let us hang life on the line, as painters say, and look at it honestly.

Seen in their true relations, there is no experience of life over which one has a right to worry. Ruskin says, "God gives us always strength enough, and sense enough for everything he wants us to do." Sense enough: this thought comforts me. It is not the lack of ability that often worries us; it is the lack of a little *savoir faire*. It is not our failures that distress us so much as our idiocies.

We may let go discontent. In all the eternal years there is no word of murmur from any restless heart. In its vast silences how trivial would sound the complainings of our harassed days! In its great songs of praise how our frettings would be overborne!

In life I find two things that make for discontent. One is lack of harmony with one's environment. The other is dissatisfaction with one's present opportunities. Of these, the first may be overcome; the second may be put out of one's life. A congenial environment is not one of the essentials of life: present opportunities, if rightly used, are as great as the soul need ask. Which of us can sit down at the close of a day and say, Today I have done all that was in my power to do for humanity and righteousness? Ah, no! We look for large things, and forget that which is close at hand! To take life "as God gives it, not as we want it," and then make the best of it, is the hard lesson that life puts before the human soul to learn.

One's environment may be very disagreeable. It may bring constant hurts of heart, mortification, tears, angry rebellion, and wounded pride, — but there is a reason for that environment. To become strong, the soul must needs fight something, overcome something. It cannot gain muscle on a bed of eider-down. A great part of the strength of life consists in the degree with which we get into harmony with our appointed environment. So long as we are at war with our town, our relatives, our family, our station, and our surroundings, so long will much of the force of our lives be spent uselessly, aimlessly. A good way to get into harmony with one's environment is to try to understand it first, and then to begin to adapt ourselves to it, so far as may be possible. "We can never work well while there is friction in our lives, nor gain in our work that " beauty which is born of power, and the sympathy which is born of love " of which Ruskin speaks.

Let us say, God put me among these scenes, these people, these opportunities, these duties. He is neither absent-minded nor incompetent. This is exactly the place He means me to be in, the place I am capable of filling: there is no mistake. My life is in its proper setting.

But with this thought in mind, we need not sit down in idleness. There are things in the circumstances of our lives that we can change; there are opportunities that our own efforts may enlarge. We can conquer many of the difficulties that beset our career, and, so conquering, be strong! I believe more and more that there is *no* impediment that cannot be overcome, *no* hindrance to usefulness that cannot be removed. If we go through life timidly, weakly, ineffectively, the fault is neither with our endowment nor our environment. It is with ourselves. It is we that are not competent for life; we that are lazy, cowardly, idle. When one sets himself to live a grand life, man cannot interrupt him, God will not!

As for our opportunities, we can make a heroic life out of whatever is set before us to work with or upon. Dr. Miller tells of a poor artist who was regally entertained in a castle. He had nothing with which to repay his friends. But he shut himself up in his room for some days before he left them, locking the door, and refusing to come out, or to let anyone in. When he went away the servant found the sheets of his bed missing, and thought that he must have stolen them. But in searching further they were found in one corner of the room, and when unrolled were discovered to have a glorious picture of Alexander in the tent of Darius painted upon them.

Carlyle says, "The Situation that has not its Duty, its Ideal, was never yet occupied by man. Yes, here, in this poor, miserable, hampered, despicable Actual, wherein thou even now standest, here or nowhere is thy Ideal: work it out therefrom; and working, believe, live, be free. Fool! the Ideal is in thyself, the impediment too is in thyself: thy Condition is but the stuff thou art to shape that same Ideal out of: what matters whether such stuff be of this sort or that, so the form thou give it be heroic, be poetic ? O thou that pinest in the imprisonment of the Actual, and criest bitterly to the gods for a kingdom wherein to rule and create, know this of a truth: the thing thou seekest is already within thee, ' here or nowhere, couldst thou only see! "

If an artist can paint a great picture on a bedsheet, can we not find opportunity and material in our present environment for the thing we wish to do ?

We may let go of self-seeking. In the eternal life there is no greed. One hears of neither "mine" nor "thine." All things are for all. As the waters fled away from Tantalus, so do the good things of life flee from the grasping and selfish spirit. The richest experiences of life never come to those who try to win them selfishly. If they do gain their desires, they find them as ashes to the taste. But all blessings are in the way of him who, forgetful of self, tries to be helpful to the world, and who spends his life in loving deeds.

Pretence, worry, discontent, and self-seeking, — these are the things that we may let go. Now what are the things in life that are worthwhile? — that we should lay hold of, keep, guard, use?

It is worthwhile to be wise in the use of time. In the eternal life there is no waste of years. It is with time that we purchase everything that life has of good. It is by the wise use of time that we make ourselves competent for eternity. The most reckless spendthrift in the world is the one who squanders time. Money lost may be regained, friendships broken may be renewed, houses and lands may be sold or buried or burnt, but may be bought or gained or built again. But what power can restore the moment that has passed, the day whose sun has set, the year that has been numbered with the ages gone?

It awes me when I think of it, that there was a time when you and I were not; — when the cycles of eternity swept onward and the stars turned in their courses without the sight or sound of man. And then came a time when Tubal Cain worked at his brasses, and Job watched Orion from the plain of Shinar, — and yet you and I were not. But now there can never come a time when you and I shall not be. The vast gift of eternity has been laid in your hands and mine: an eternity not wholly to come, but one which is even now here. Shall we not use its hours aright?

The question of life is not, How much time have we? — for in each day each of us has exactly the same amount: we have "all there is." The question is, What shall we do with it? Shall we let this priceless gift slip away from us in haphazard deeds, or shall we adopt some plan of saving and of systematic doing in our lives? What shall this plan be? How shall we determine what things are worth giving time to? Let us think about this question. In our thoughts, let us not forget one point, — time spent in being interrupted is not time lost. A strong thinker once said, "No one knocks at my door who is not sent by God." We are spending time well when we are paying it out to God, to buy the things he means our lives to own, whether he is putting before us a duty to be done, a friend to be won, a small service to be rendered, a book to be written, a child to be consoled, or a house to be set in order. There is time enough given us to do all that God means us to do each day and to do it gloriously! How do we know but that the interruption we snarl at is the most blessed thing that has come to us in long days?

But in all our lives, though time is given us to eat, drink, sleep, work, and play, there is no moment given us to throw away. We have to meet this question of the wise use of time not only as individuals: we should consider it today as it affects us as an association, and our united power for good in the world. We are working out a problem in history, and the world is looking on to see what we will do with our college-trained lives, now that we have them. We cannot afford to lose a moment of usefulness, or the sum of our influence will be less than it might have been. Suppose each of us should resolve to-day that not a minute henceforward should ever be wasted. What energy there would be in our lives! What strength! What noble purpose! What grand results! What could we not accomplish as an association,

if no one of us ever lost time in grieving, in dreaming, in regret, in harmful pleasures, in idle talk! Eternity is long: there will be time enough for dreams. But life is for work and for patience. Let each of us ask herself to-day, How much am I going to deduct from the grand possible total of time in our lives, by my idleness, my unthrift?

Let us lay hold of work. There can be no happy life without strenuous, unremitting work in it,— work which occupies mind, body, heart, and soul. But what work shall we set ourselves to do? This is one of the questions that meets us when we leave college, and that reappears from time to time as we see more of the possibilities of life. We fear to make mistakes! We do not want to throw our powers away; to build walls of sand when we might have built "monuments more lasting than bronze."

There are three questions that we may ask about a work before we decide to take it up. Is it legitimate? Is it individual? Is it vital? How many kinds of work an honest answer to these questions would cut out at once! By legitimate I mean, Does it conflict with any present known duty? If so, that work is not for our hands to do. If we attempt it we are leaving our duty undone, and are become a busybody in other men's matters. By individual I mean, Is it a work that belongs to me alone? It is a wonderful truth, that no one of us is put into life without a special and particular work to do. Emerson says, "Nature arms each man with some faculty which enables him to do easily some feat impossible to any other." How true this is! In all the universe of God there are no two souls alike. There are no two with the same work to do. There are no two whose talents are rivals, or whose gifts conflict or interfere. How this thought ought to put an end at once to all the envy of life,— grieving at another's good! His good is not my good. It was never meant to be. I could not gain it if I tried. On the other hand, what I can do my neighbor cannot. Why should either of us be jealous of the other, or imagine that we conflict? Each human soul can say, I am unique. In all the worlds and worlds, in all the ages and ages, there has never been any one like me, and in all time there shall never be again. I have no double.

Is the work vital? Is it of eternal moment, either in strengthening my own character, or inspiring others, or helping the world? If so, the work is worth doing.

We are all capitalists. The only pauper in the world is a

dumb, deaf, and blind idiot. Let us examine our capacities and gifts, and then put them to the best use we may. As our own view of life is of necessity partial, I do not find that we can do better than to put them absolutely in God's hand, and look to him for the direction of our life-energy. God can do great things with our lives, if we but give them to him in sincerity. He can make them useful, uplifting, heroic. God never wastes anything. God never forgets anything. God never loses anything. Though He holds the worlds in the hollow of his hand, He will yet remember each of us, and the part we are fitted to play in the eternal drama.

Let us not try to escape our work, nor to shirk it. Above all, let us not fail to see it. As long as we live we have a work to do. We shall never be too old for it, nor too feeble. Illness, weakness, fatigue, sorrow,— none of these thing can excuse us from this work of ours. That we are alive to-day is proof positive that God has something for us to do to-day. Let us ask ourselves as we arise each morning, What is my work to-day? We do not know where the influence of to-day will end. Our lives may outgrow all our present thoughts, and outdazzle all our dreams. Every day is a test day; every hour is an examination-hour. God puts each fresh morning, each new chance of life, into our hands as a gift, to see what we will do with it. A servant takes a block of wood and throws it into the fire: Gasparo Becerra seizes it from the flame, and carves from it an immortal statue. As Dr. Trumbull says, "Today is, for all that we know, the opportunity and occasion of our lives. On what we do or say today may depend the success and completeness of our entire life-struggle. It is for us, therefore, to use every moment of to-day as if our very eternity were dependent on its words and deeds."

If we do not do the work we were meant to do, it will forever remain undone. In the annals of eternity there will be some good lacking that we might have provided, some reward unbestowed that we might have had: there will be something incomplete in all the everlasting years. Oh, the sorrow of opportunities neglected, slighted, or despised! Oh, the remorse for the good we might have done, and did not! Do they not bring regret and pain to the sensitive soul?

Again, this work of ours, whatever it may be, will never pass away. We are a part of the great world-energy: no atom of its force is ever lost. Every breath of our lives, every noble heart-beat, will pulsate through all eternity. Our lives are indelible, imperishable.

Let us lay hold of the happiness of to-day. Do we not go through life blindly, thinking that some fair to-morrow will bring us the gift we miss to-day? Poor mortal, when thinkest thou then to be happy? Tomorrow? What is tomorrow? How is it different from today? Is it not but another to-day? Know thou, my heart, if thou art not happy to-day, thou shalt never be happy! To-day it is given thee to be patient, to be unselfish, to be purposeful, to be strong, eager, and to work mightily! If thou

doest these things, and if, remembering all thy mercies, thou doest them with a grateful heart, thou shalt be happy,— at least, as happy as it is given man to be on earth. When all is said and done, when the shades of twilight fall, and thou sayest, I have had a happy day, is there not something yet beyond it all, deeper than all, and more satisfying, towards which the heart turns with sad longing, as of a child for its mother's breast? This is the yearning of life, the cry for the fullness of eternity, which shall be stilled only in the presence of God: it is not for us here below.

What thou callest happiness, —is it not often a certain fall in the thermometer, bringing cool winds and a fresh air? Is it not a question of sun, or of kind words said to thee of affection or sympathy, or of success in some trifle of thy business? Are these things, then, happiness? Do they satisfy forever thy soul? Not so! Thou art happy when thou hast done thy duty, be the skies dark or fair, be men kind or unkind, just or base. Thou art happy when thou hast done what God has planned for thee this day, this hour: when thou hast been brave, helpful, and above all uncomplaining of thy lot!

Let us lay hold of common duties and relations. Let us lay hold of the tenderness that belongs to them. Shall we miss all the divine sweetness of life in order to have a career? Shall we shed home, family, relatives, and domestic duties, in order to learn Sanskrit, ethnology, philology? Not all college-bred women think how that sounds when, led by no pressure of bread-winning which impels them to seek higher advantages, but simply by an absorbing ambition, they leave their father or mother, or both, in a lonely home. Let us consider life at all points before we rush into a new phase of it, from which, once in, we may not soon withdraw.

This is the great danger, and a grave one it is, that is apt, at some time or other, to confront us all,— the danger of substituting some intellectual ambition for the ordinary human affections. I do not know how to speak strongly enough on this subject, and yet gently enough. It is on my heart night and day, as I consider our common problem. Ambition is, in many ways, the most deadly foe we have,— the most deadly foe to our character I mean. Little by little that intellectual ambition will draw us away, if we are not careful, from our true place in life, and will make cold, unloved, and unhelpful women of us, instead of the joyous, affectionate, and unselfish women we might have been. We need not try to annihilate ambition, but let us keep it in bounds; let us see to it that it holds a just proportion in our lives. We need not let our talents lie idle, nor neglect to make the most of them; there is a place and a grand work for them all; but let us keep their development forever subordinate to simple human duties, usually at home. Very few lives are free,— free to go and come, travel, read, study, write, think, paint, sing, at will. In the lives of most women these gifts are an aside in life, as it were, an underbreath. Most of us are beset with loving calls of toil, care, responsibility, and quiet duties, which we must recognize, heed, obey.

We must love our mothers more than Greek dialects. If the instinct of daughter, sister, wife, or mother dies out of a college-bred woman, even in the course of a most brilliant career otherwise, the world will forget to love her; it will scorn her, and justly. If she does not make her surroundings home-like wherever she is, whether she be teacher, artist, musician, doctor, writer, daughter at home, or a mother in her household, and if she herself is not cheery and loving, dainty in dress, gentle in manner, and beautiful in soul as every true woman ought to be, the world will feel that the one thing needful is lacking, — vivid, tender womanliness, for which no knowledge of asymptotes or linguistics can ever compensate. It is better for a woman to fill a simple human part lovingly, better for her to be sympathetic in trouble and to whisper a comforting message into but one grieving ear, than that she should make a path to Egypt and lecture to thousands on ancient Thebes.

Let us lay hold of friendship. In the eternal life shall we not have friends forevermore? I used to think that friendship meant happiness: I have learned that it means discipline. Seek how we may, we shall never find a friend without faults, imperfections, traits, and ways that vex, grieve, annoy us. Strive as we will, we ourselves can never fully fulfill the ideal of us that is in our friend's mind: we inevitably come short of it. Yet let us not give up friendship, though we have found this true. To have a friend is to have one of the sweetest gifts that life can bring: to be a friend is to have a solemn and tender education of soul from day to day. A friend gives us confidence for life. A friend makes us outdo ourselves. A friend remembers us when we have forgotten ourselves, or neglected ourselves: he takes loving heed of our health, our work, our aims, our plans. A friend may praise us, and we are not embarrassed; he may rebuke us, and we are not angered. If he be silent, we understand. It takes a great soul to be a true friend,— a large, catholic, steadfast, and loving spirit. One must forgive much, forget much, forbear much. It costs to be a friend, or to have a friend: there is nothing else in life, except motherhood, that costs so much. It not only costs time, affection, strength, patience, love,— sometimes a man must even lay down his

WHAT IS WORTH WHILE?

life for his friends. There is no true friendship without self-abnegation, self-sacrifice.

Let us be slow to make friends, but, having once made them, let us pray that neither life nor death, misunderstanding, distance, nor doubt, may ever come between us, to vex our peace. Let us be patient, let us be kindly, let us be self-possessed in friendship. There are so many ways of grieving a friend,—shall we not walk softly before him ? Let us be true to our friends, and then believe that they are and ever will be true to us. True love never nags; it trusts. One of the dearest thoughts to me is this,— that a real friend will never get away from me, or try to, or want to. Love does not have to be tethered, either in time or eternity. \ It is a great and solemn thing to say to another human soul, In this one life that we have to live, we will share all things temporal and spiritual. Your joys shall be my joys. Your sorrows shall be my sorrows. In absence you shall yet be near. You shall never be so far from me but that I can hear your voice in the twilight and in the night-season. Though land and sea divide us, you shall yet walk by my side and kneel with me in prayer; still I shall feel the touch of your hand, and rejoice in your sympathy. Your letters shall make me strong and glad. I am not afraid of you. With you I need not be too greatly reserved. To you I may speak the deep thoughts of my heart. With you alone I laugh; with you only may I shed tears and be not ashamed. To you only can I say, " Behold, here am I, an undisguised human soul: all others know me in some one mood,— you know me in all moods." '

In the eternal life we may make new friends: I dare say we

shall. But can those radiant, perfect, and glorified ones ever be quite so near and dear to us as those more human souls that we have known when they, like ourselves, were but struggling, aspiring, and suffering mortals; those who have shared joy and pain with us, who have watched us wistfully over mountain, wilderness, and sea, who have quarreled with us and kissed us again, who have loved us with tenderness, and who have been faithful to us, even unto death? Meetings and partings, handclasps and farewells, loving nearness and grieving tears,— these are the lot of friendship on earth. But in eternity there shall be neither weeping nor any sound of sighing, and there shall be no parting there.

Let us lay hold of sorrow. Let us not be afraid of it, for when grasped firmly, like the nettle, it never stings. The life that has not known and accepted sorrow is strangely crude and untaught. It can neither help nor teach, for it has never learned. The life that has spurned the lesson of sorrow, or failed to read it aright, is cold and hard; but the life that has been disciplined by sorrow is courageous, and full of holy and gentle love. Without sorrow life glares. It has no half-tones nor merciful shadows. Disappointment, in life, is inevitable. Pain is the common lot of humanity. Sharp sorrow, at one time or another, will come to each of us, if indeed it has not already come. But this same sorrow is a gentle teacher, and reveals many things that would otherwise be hard to understand.

Sorrow passes. "See," says a keen observer, " how little trace a single sorrow, even a great one, leaves in any life." He did not mean that the influence of sorrow is slight,— he only meant that life is greater than sorrow, and need not be overborne by it. Says Emerson, " All loss, all gain, is particular: ... it is only the finite that has wrought and suffered; the infinite lies stretched in smiling repose."

There is no new sorrow. We shall be called upon to bear nothing that has not been borne before. Does not this thought still in part the wild clamor of life ? Shall we murmur at our lot when unnumbered mourning hearts, as sensitive, as true, as loving, as our own, have been breaking under the weight of the same sorrow that oppresses us to-day, have met this grief of ours, whatever it may be, and have conquered it ? Shall we not rather now in turn try to bear the cross more bravely than any that have gone before, that we may give strength and courage to the weary ones who must bear it after us? Every day of meeting sorrow superbly makes the life more grand. Every tear that falls from one's own eyes gives a deeper tenderness of look, of touch, of word, that shall soothe another's woe. Sorrow is not given to us alone that we may mourn. It is given us, that, having felt, suffered, wept, we may be able to understand, love, bless.

Let us lay hold of faith. Of what profit is it to us to gain a firm hold on life, if we hold it but blindly, without any light on the meaning of our present condition, or the character of our future destiny? Faith, Christian faith, holds the key to the blessedness of the eternal life. Faith opens the gate of pearl, and lets us in. Strong, serene, unquenchable faith in the loving-kindness of God, the wisdom of Providence, the guidance of the Holy Spirit, and the redeeming love of Christ, will enable us to look fearlessly toward the end of the temporal existence and the beginning of the eternal, and will make it possible for us to live our lives effectively, grandly! Letting go the unworthy things that meet us, pretense, worry, discontent and self-seeking, — and taking loyal hold of time, work, present happiness, love, duty, friendship, sorrow, and faith, let us so live in all true womanliness as to be an inspiration, strength, and blessing to those whose lives are touched by ours!

SHORT ESSAYS THAT CHANGED THE WORLD

Some of history's most powerful writings were not hundreds of pages long. Brief, potent works have played an outsized role in shaping thought, values, and society itself. In the 19th and early 20th centuries, short essays and pamphlets electrified the public, bringing new philosophies, exposures of injustice, and calls for change.

Thinkers like Ralph Waldo Emerson, Henry David Thoreau, John Stuart Mill, and John Ruskin could condense world-shaking ideas into potent works spanning just a few dozen pages. Sometimes discretely published, other times appearing in magazines or newspapers, these short works embedding themselves into the culture and conversation of their era. Their brevity belied their influence.

While we may think of influence today in terms of viral posts or tweetstorms, we can look back and see how a few thousand well-chosen words permanently shifted paradigms. These essays highlighted foundational values, exposed hypocrisy, and brought enlightening ideas to broader audiences. Their standout clarity and conviction brought generations of readers onboard with their messages.

This short book is just one of a number of essays written the early 1800s and 1900s that:

- Offered philosophical visions for life,
- Created new social justice movements,
- Revealed injustices that demanded remedy, and
- Literally flew from hand to hand, becoming catalysts for change.

Following is an overview of other short essays which, like "What is Worth While?" by Anna Robertson Brown Lindsay, not only changed the world at that time, but continue to shape it today:

"A Message to Garcia" by Elbert Hubbard (1899)

This brief inspirational essay promoted individual initiative and resourcefulness. It told the story of a soldier who reliably delivered a message without needing instructions. It circulated widely after its publication, including being printed as a pamphlet by various corporations. The essay's praise of hard work and initiative resonated in the business world.

"A Vindication of the Rights of Woman" by Mary Wollstonecraft (1792)

This was an early landmark feminist essay advocating for the equality and education of women. Wollstonecraft argued women were capable of rational thought and should receive the same educational opportunities as men. She refuted common arguments that women were inferior. The essay helped ignite the 19th century women's rights movement and remains an important philosophical work on gender equality.

"Civil Disobedience" by Henry David Thoreau (1849)

Thoreau's essay argued individuals should follow their conscience and disobey unjust laws. He advocated principled resistance through civil disobedience and nonviolent protest. It had a deep influence on later activists including Gandhi and Martin Luther King Jr. The essay remains one of the most influential defenses of conscientious objection.

"Classical Economics" by Henry George (1898)

This influential treatise critiqued the wealth inequality created by laissez-faire capitalism. George advocated reforms like a single tax on land ownership to fairly distribute wealth. His ideas inspired economic reform movements concerned with inequality.

"How We Think" by John Dewey (1910)

The educational philosopher outlined his principles of logical, reflective thinking and problem solving in this highly circulated work. It influenced modern pedagogy by advocating active learning experiences over rote memorization. Dewey stressed cultivating critical thinking skills.

"Self-Reliance" by Ralph Waldo Emerson (1841)

Emerson's famous essay extolled the need for nonconformity, self-reliance and personal integrity. It urged readers to think independently without blindly following social norms. The essay exemplified Emerson's belief in individualism and inspired generations of thinkers. It remains one of the most influential works of American literature.

"Shooting an Elephant" by George Orwell (1936)

Orwell's autobiographical essay criticized the evils of British imperialism. He reflected on being compelled to shoot an elephant against his conscience as a colonial police officer. The essay demonstrated Orwell's burgeoning talent for impactful political writing.

"The Immorality of Eating Meat" by Henry Stephens Salt (1886)

This early persuasive essay advocated ethical vegetarianism and animal welfare reforms. Salt argued against the cruel practices of industrialized farming. His humanitarian essay helped ignite the modern movement for vegetarianism and humane farming laws in Britain.

"The Kingdom of God Is Within You" by Leo Tolstoy (1894)

This work explained Tolstoy's Christian anarchist philosophy of nonviolence. He argued that Christianity had been corrupted by church dogma and hierarchies. Instead, he believed the Kingdom of God was based on compassion, human dignity, and peace. The book greatly impacted Gandhi and the nascent pacifist movement.

"The Souls of Black Folk" by W.E.B. Du Bois (1903)

This collection of essays exposed the systemic racism facing African Americans after the Civil War. Du Bois refuted bigoted depictions of black culture and advocated for full equality. He famously described the struggle of having a "double consciousness" in a racist society. The landmark work sparked nationwide discussion on civil rights.

"The Uses of Great Men" by Herbert Spencer (1859)

Spencer's essay argued that seminal thinkers and innovative leaders are the main drivers of human progress throughout history. He contended that great individuals introduce ideas and actions that advance civilization. The work exemplified Spencer's individualist perspective.

"Unto This Last" by John Ruskin (1862)

Ruskin's passionate critique of laissez-faire capitalism rejected harmfully competitive economic theories. He argued that an industrialized economy was dehumanizing workers and causing wealth inequality. Ruskin advocated for more humane social values like cooperation and dignity for laborers. The essay's ideas influenced later thinkers like Gandhi.

"What is Enlightenment?" by Immanuel Kant (1784)

This highly influential treatise called on people to think for themselves free from prejudice and paternalistic authority. Kant defined enlightenment as the emergence from "self-imposed immaturity" through critical thinking and intellectual courage. The essay profoundly shaped the spirit and values of the Enlightenment era.